DESIGNS FOR COLORING

SEA SHELLS

7

BY RUTH HELLER

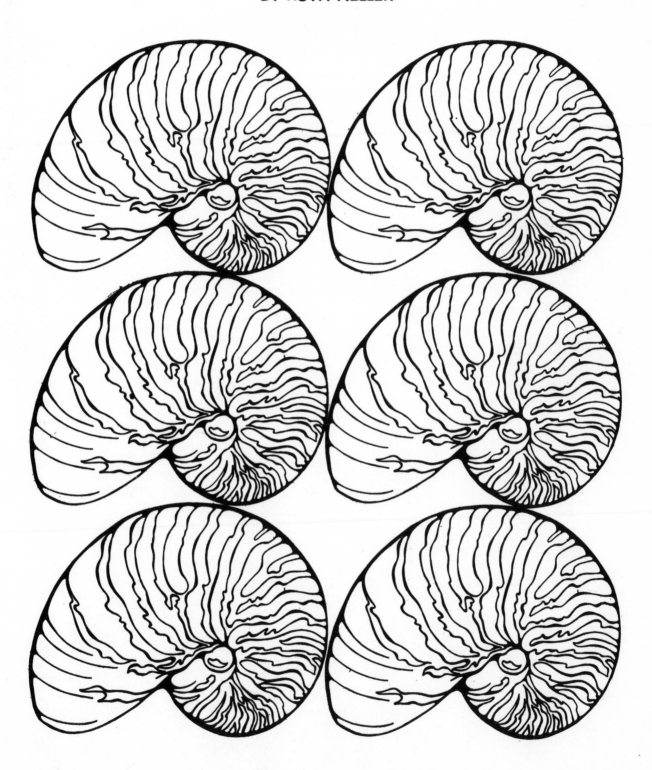

DESIGNS FOR COLORING

The seashell designs forming the many patterns in this book are much more than guidelines for the random distribution of color by crayons, pastels, felt-tipped pens, pencils, or water paints. More to the point, they are tie lines to your own imagination, the application of which will create an infinite variety of surprisingly new and different designs that range from simple to elaborate, realistic to abstract.

You can choose from single, large units filling the entire design space or select patterns that are repetitive in an allover view. You can then choose your own colors—bold bright ones for emphasis or light and subtle shades—according to your mood, or, more often, an interpretive response. You can extend your color over a large area—or restrict it—again, as you may "feel" it or "see" it. You can start where you like and you can finish where you like.

The results achieved may vary in impact, but every effort will reflect your own artistic expression. Individual. Personal. You may even want to utilize an especially eye-pleasing or decorative pattern in a transition to embroidery, needlepoint, hand-printed fabrics, ceramics, and mosaics.

Whatever the case, you will find hours of pleasure as your imagination is challenged at every turn. You cannot be too young or too old to experience a fulfilling involvement.

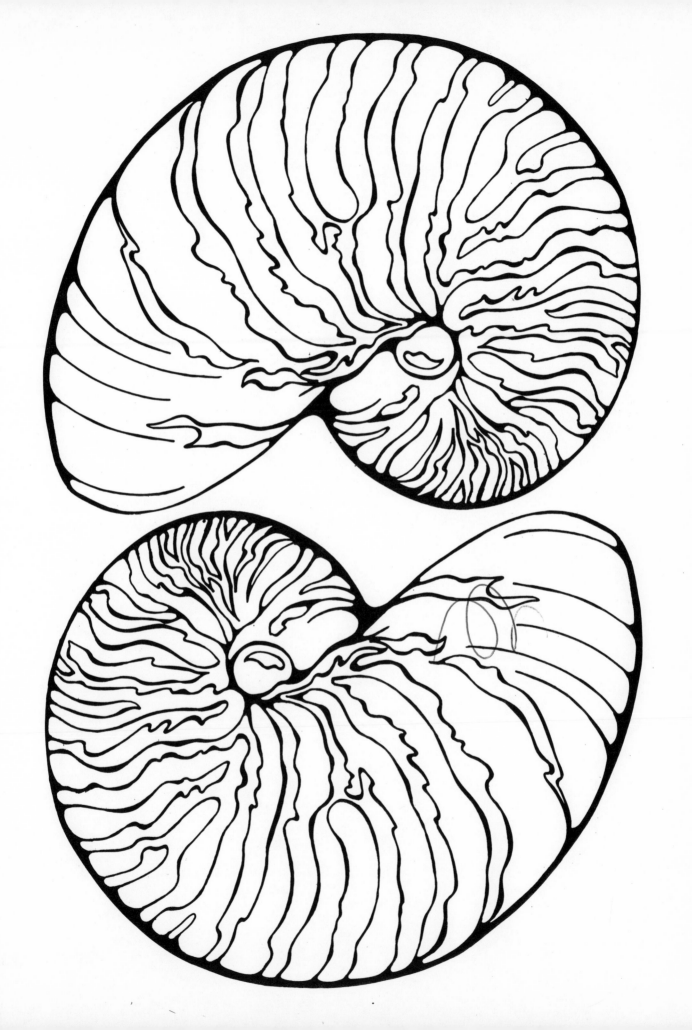

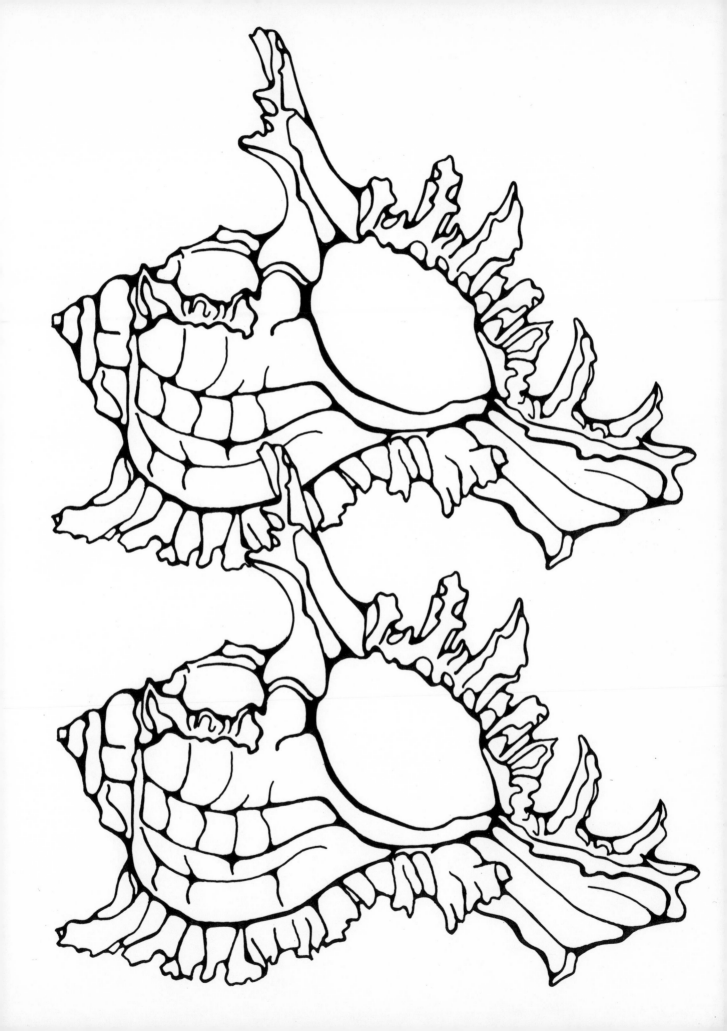

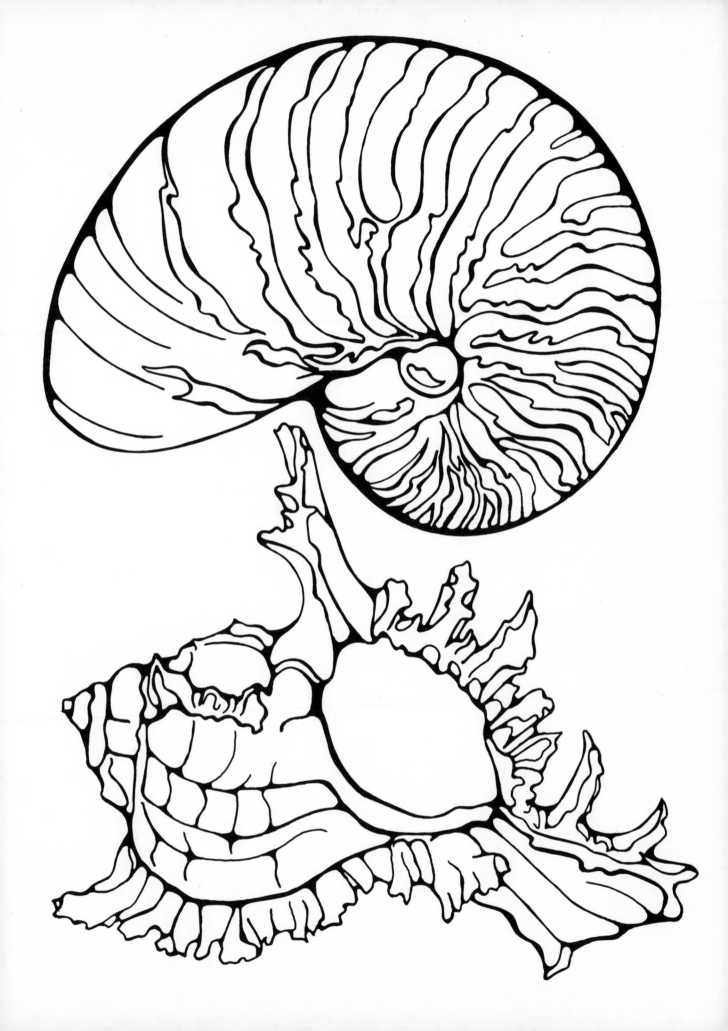

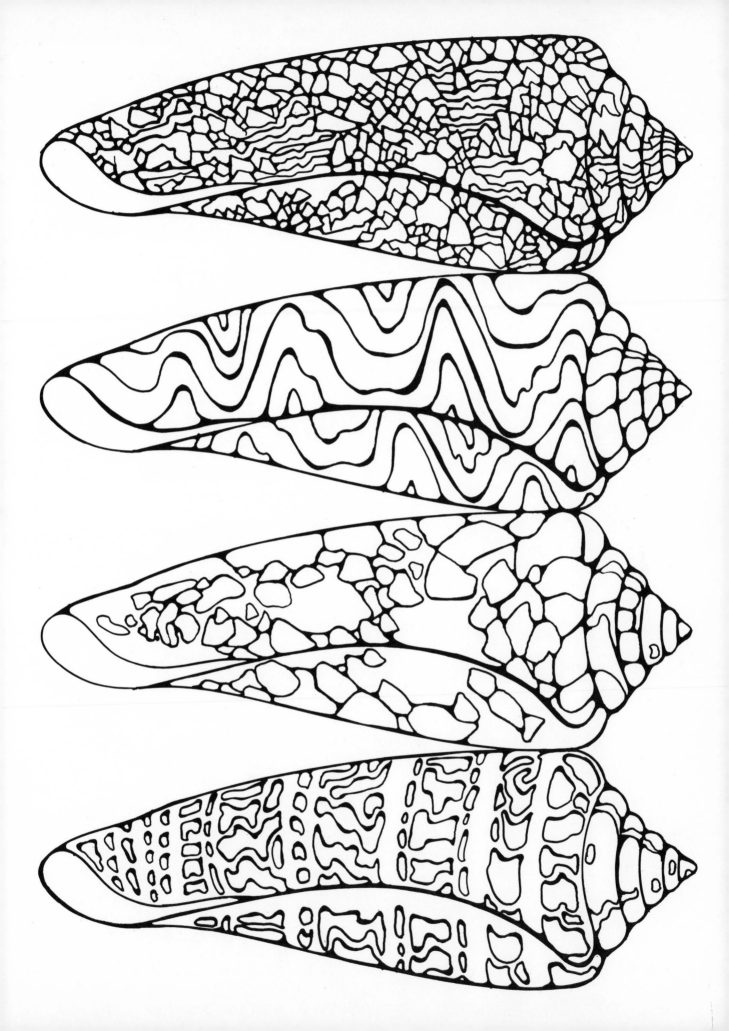

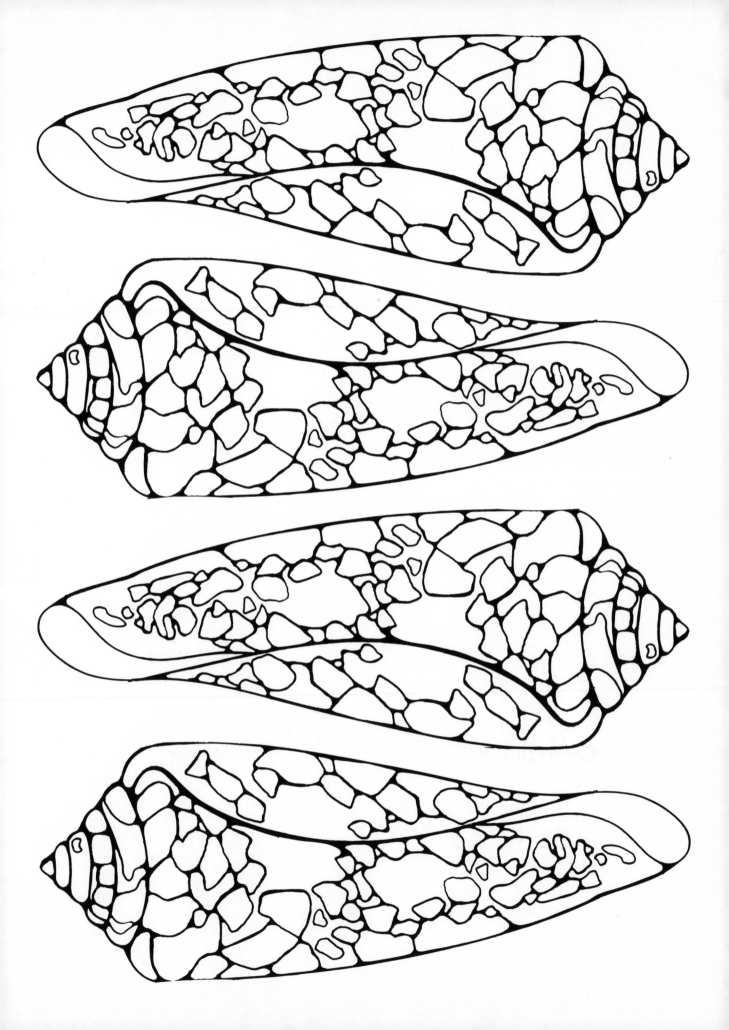

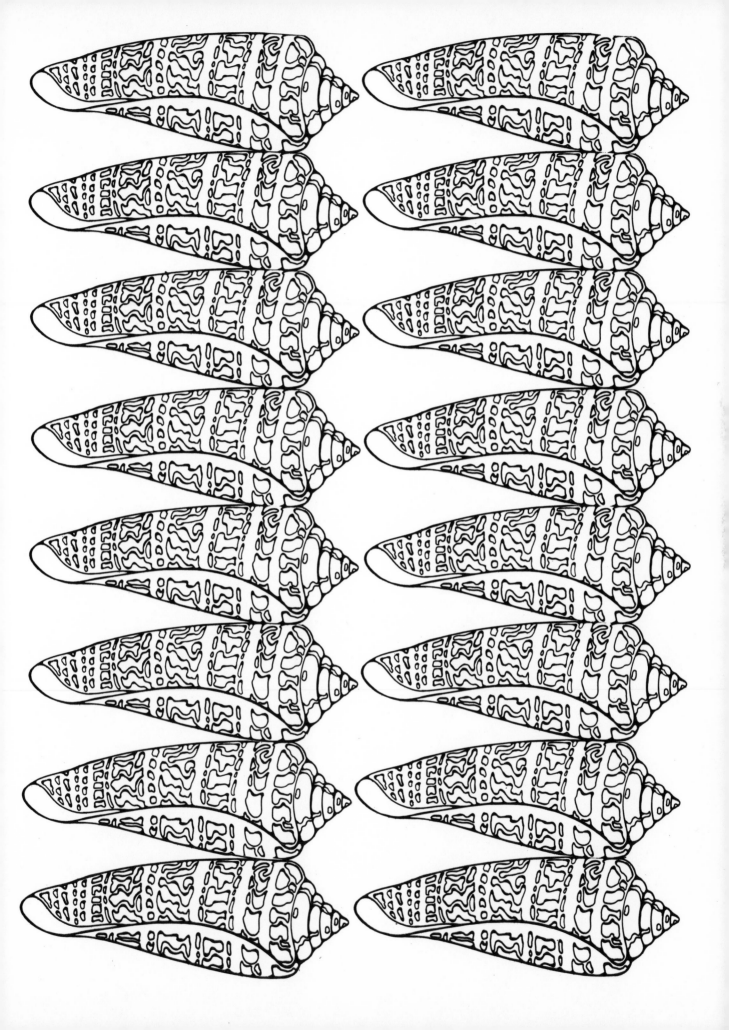

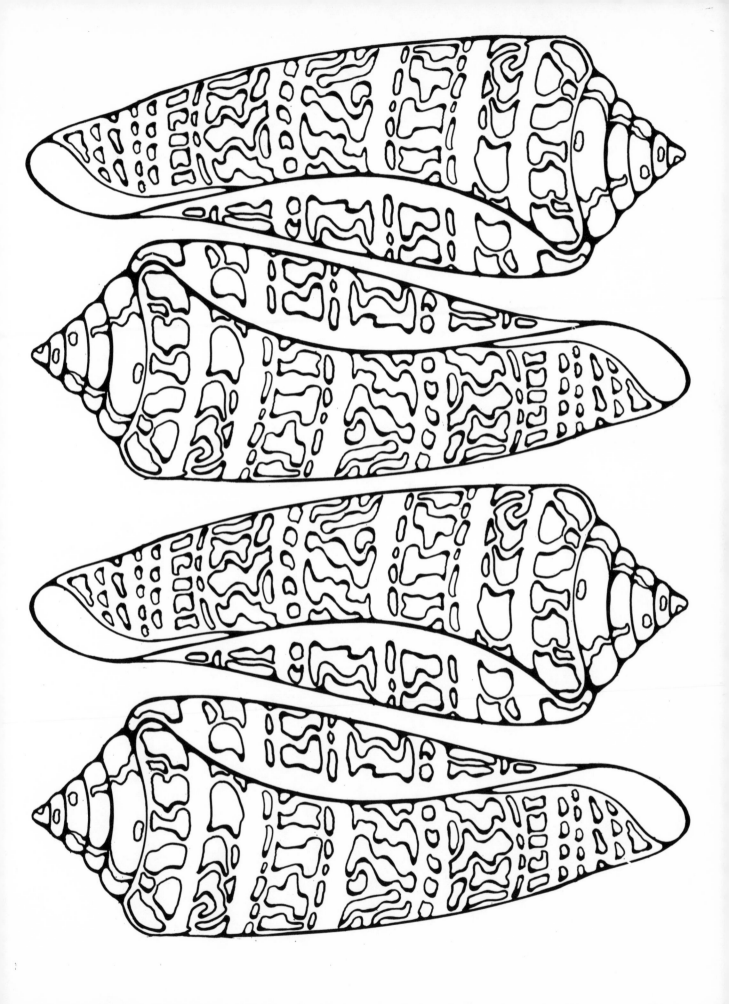

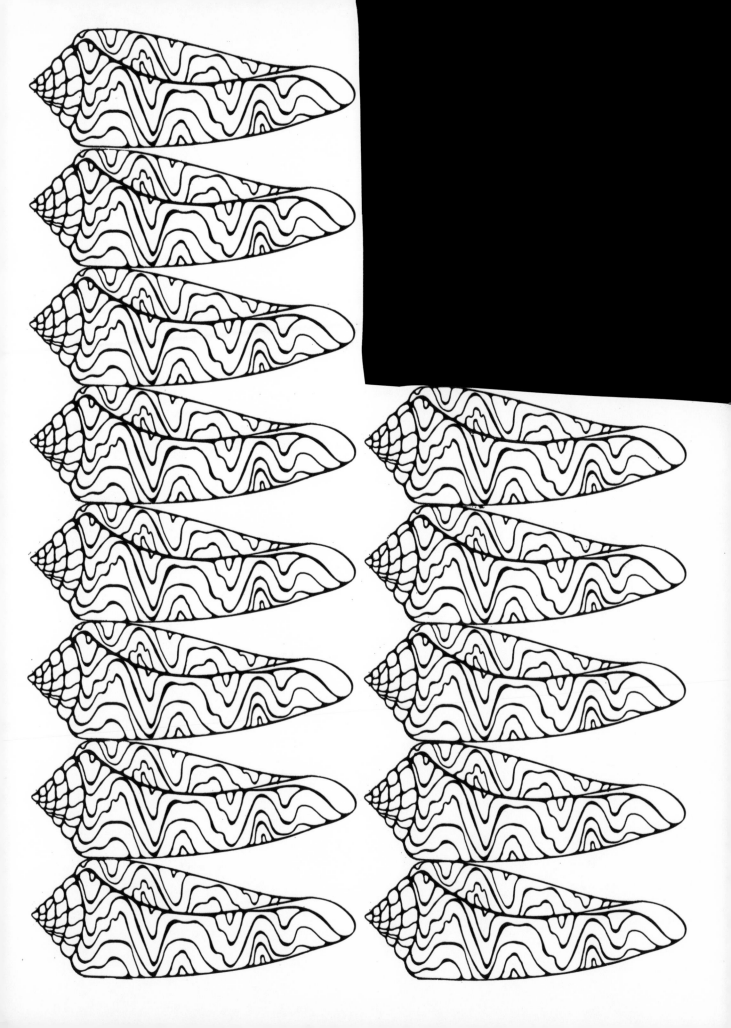

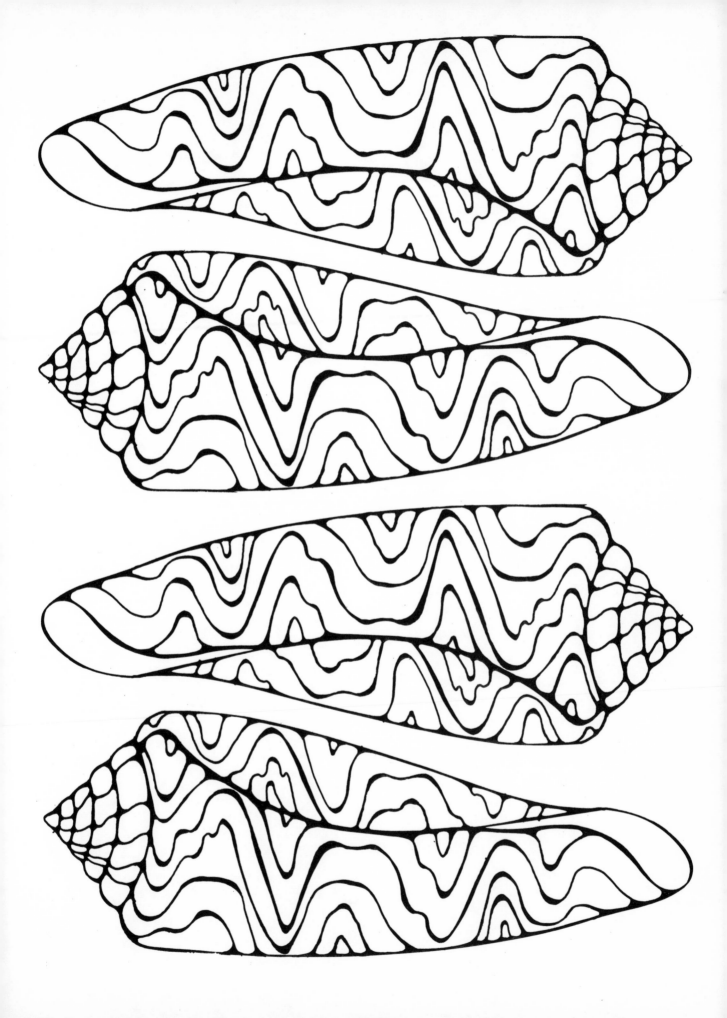

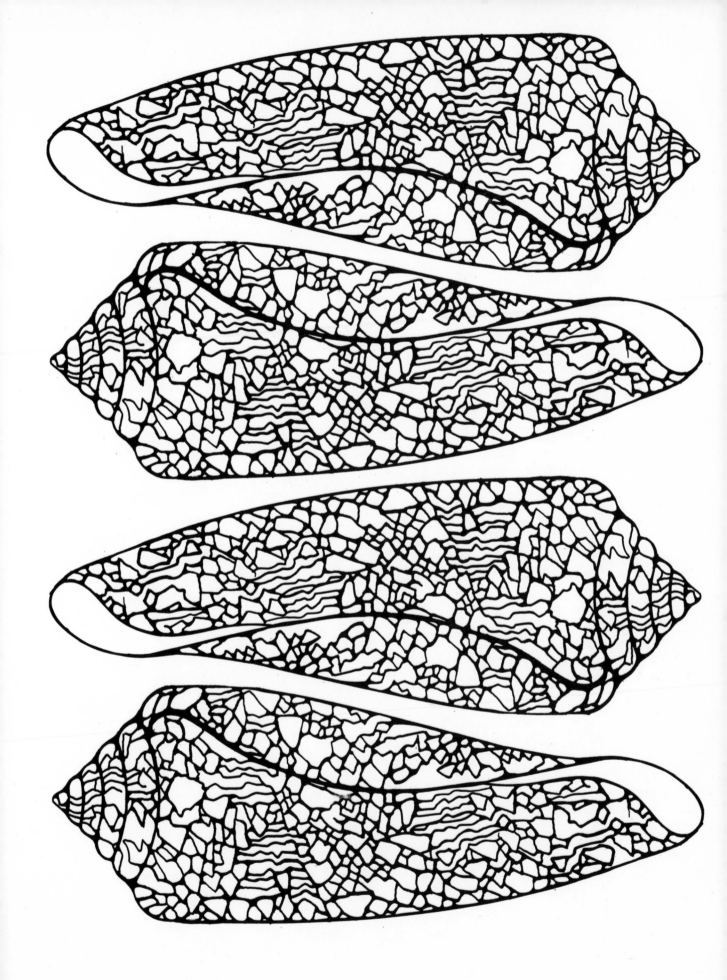

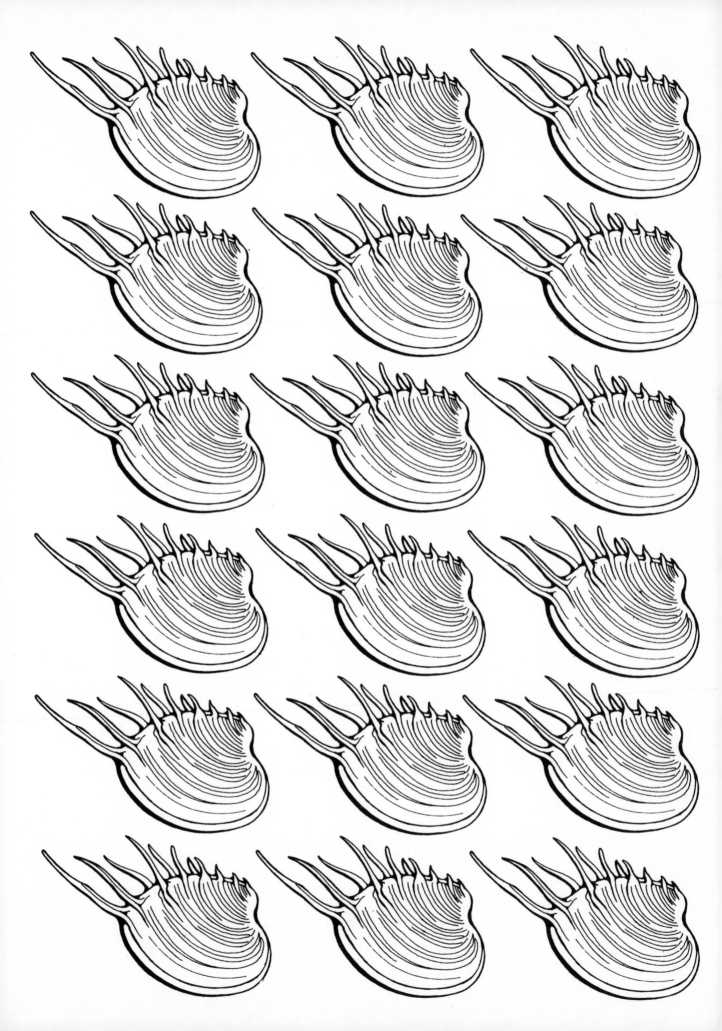

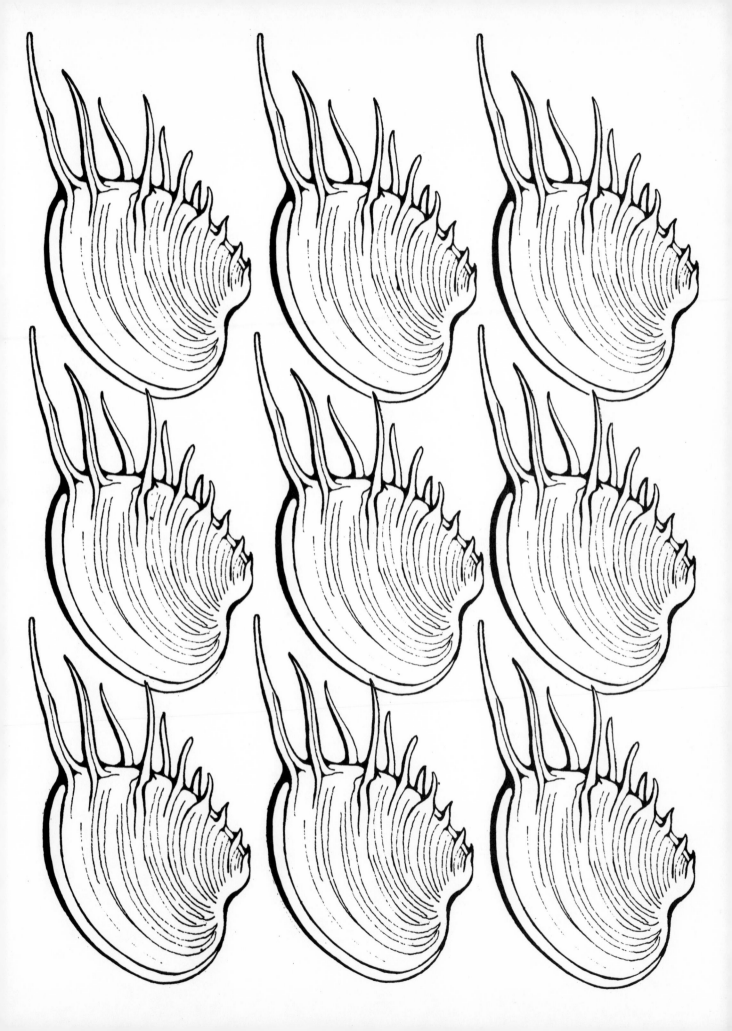

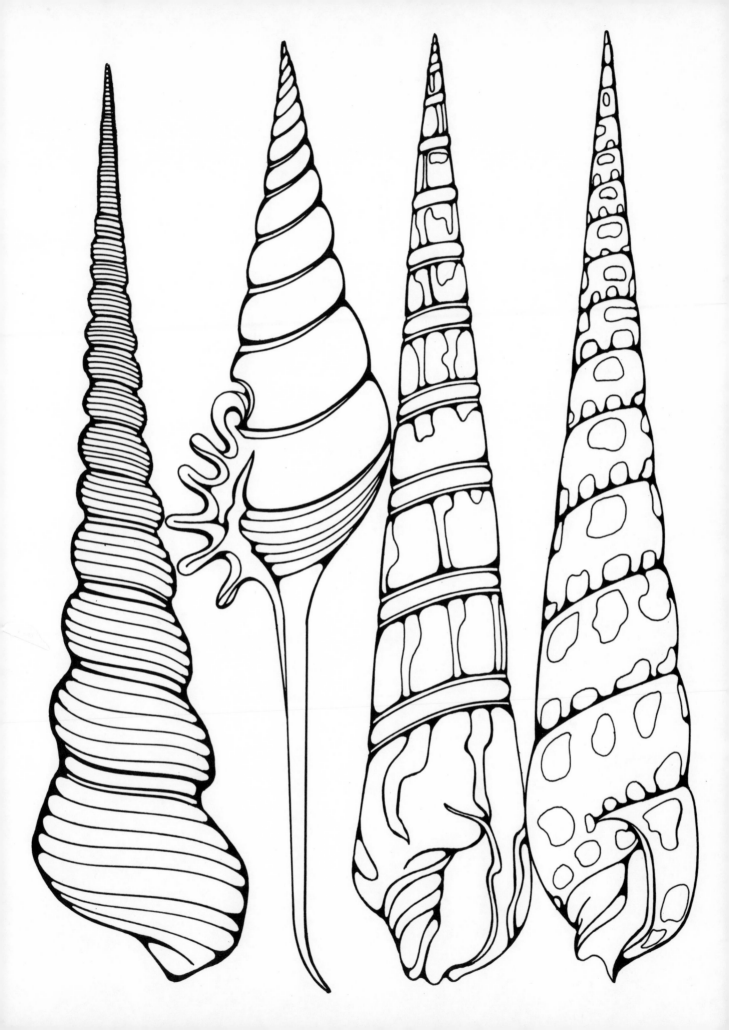

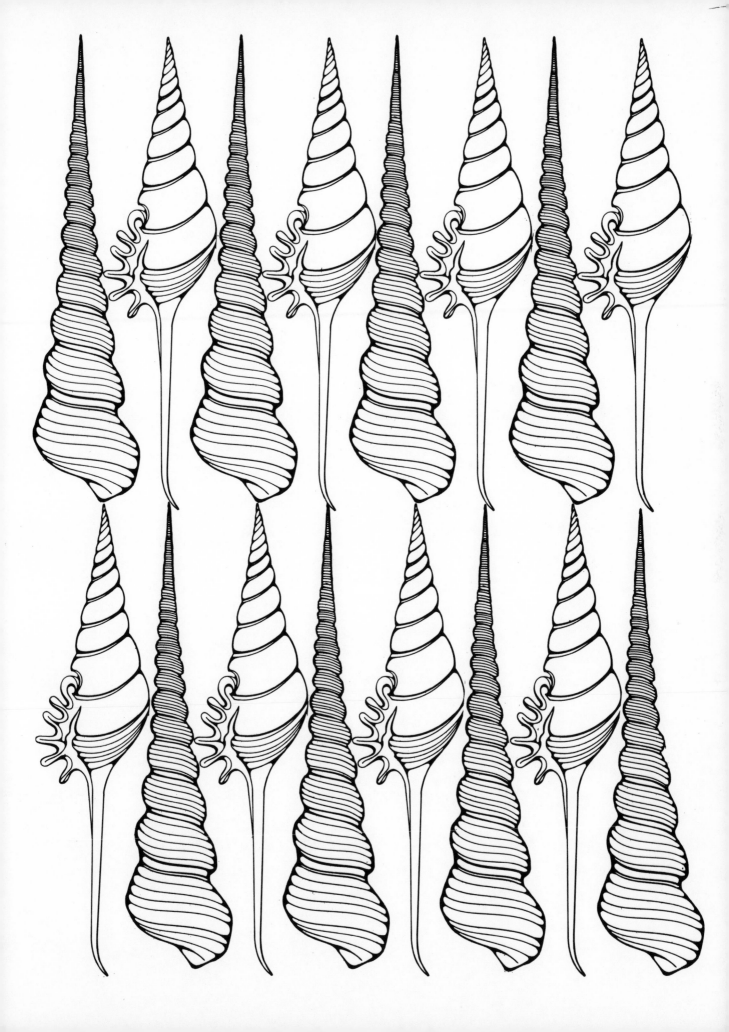

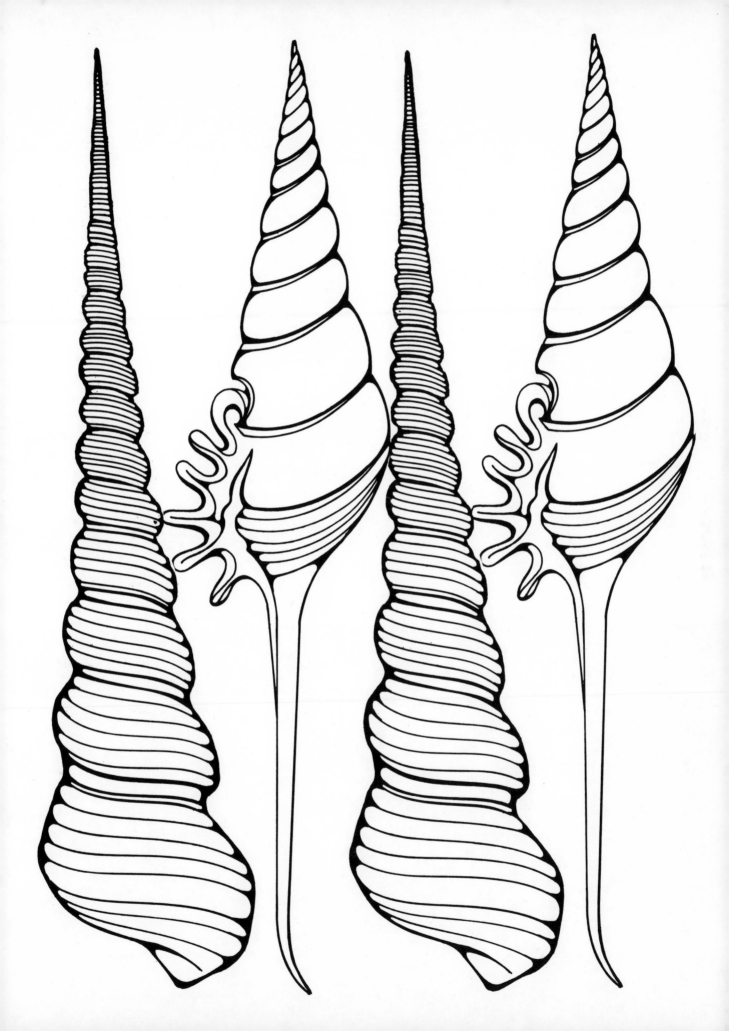

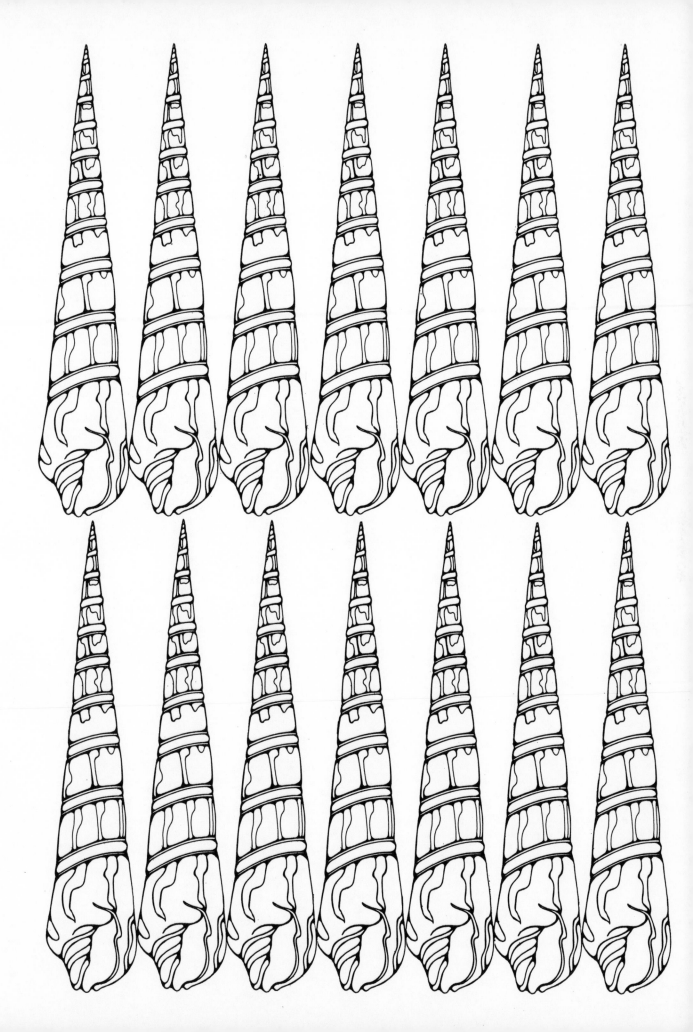

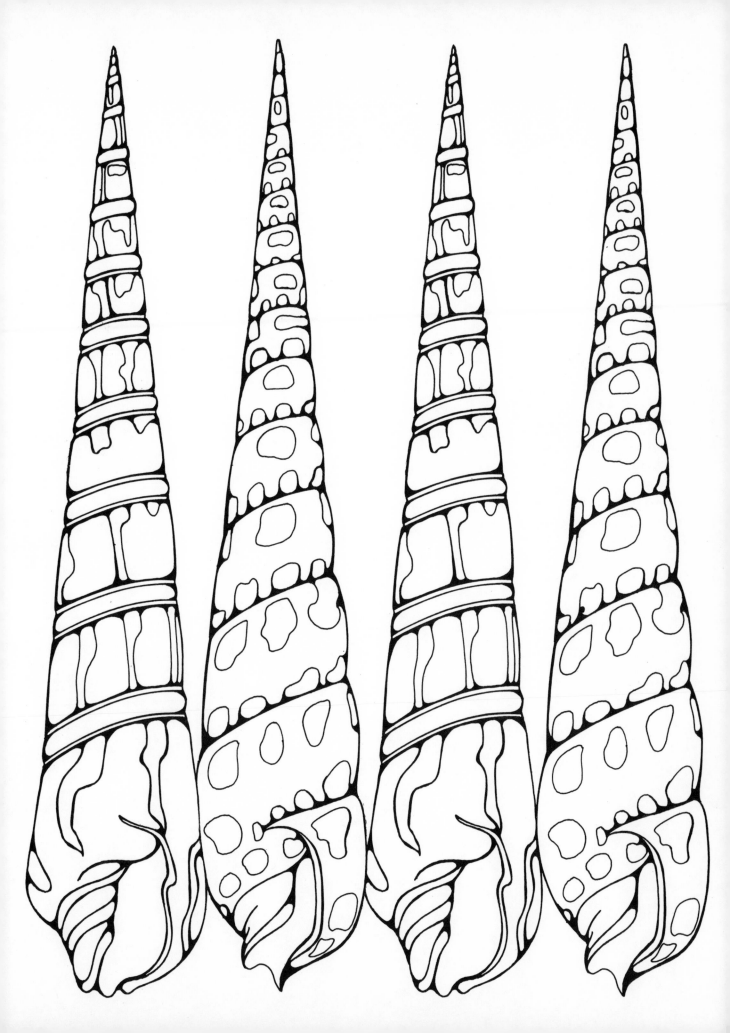

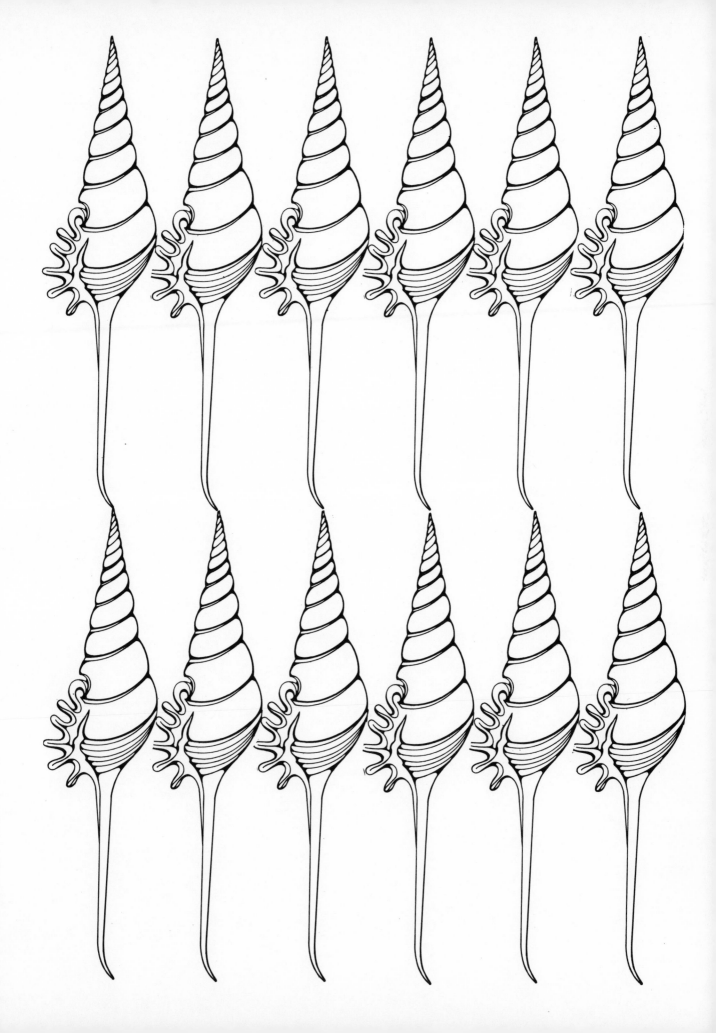

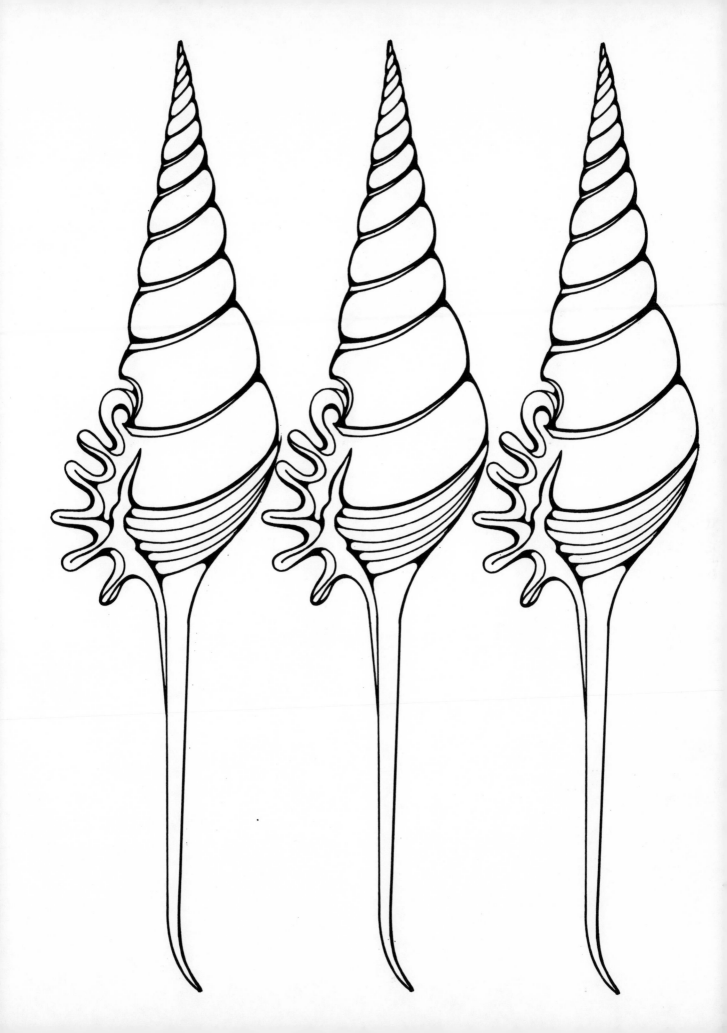

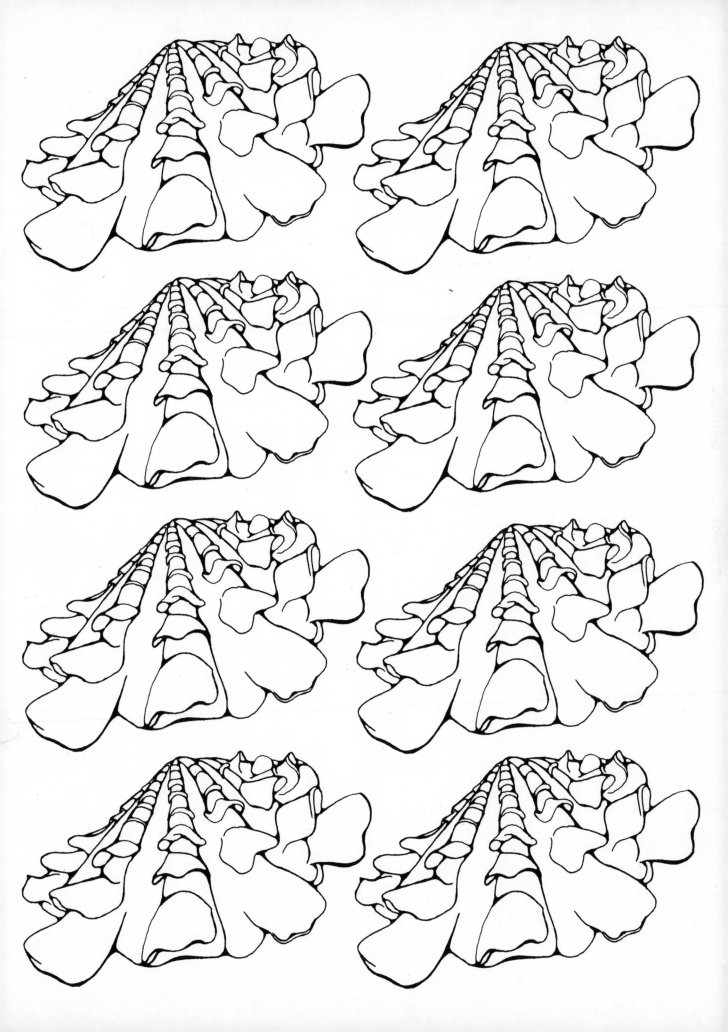

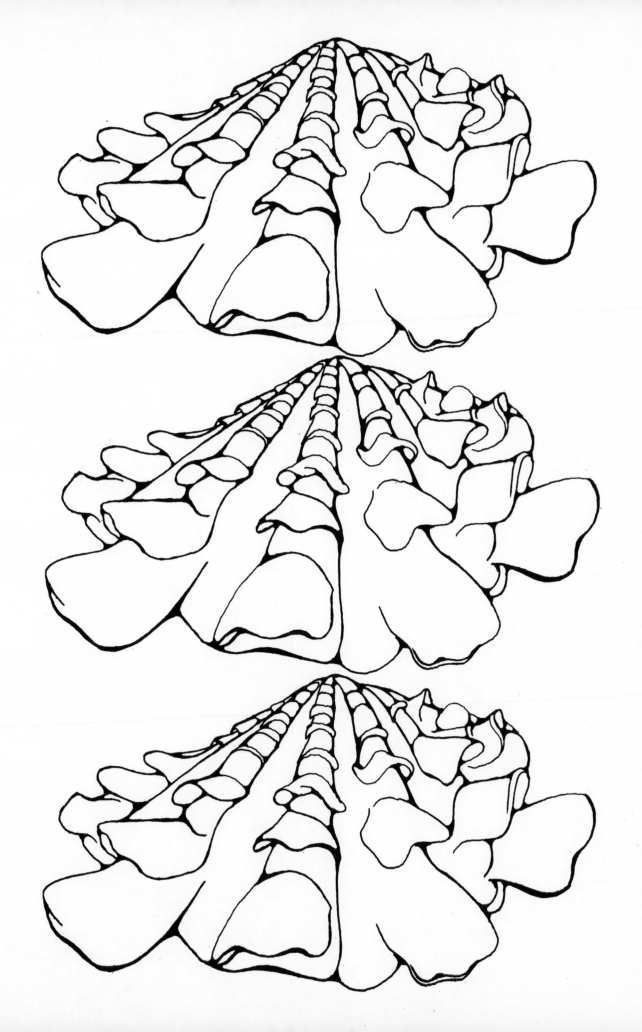

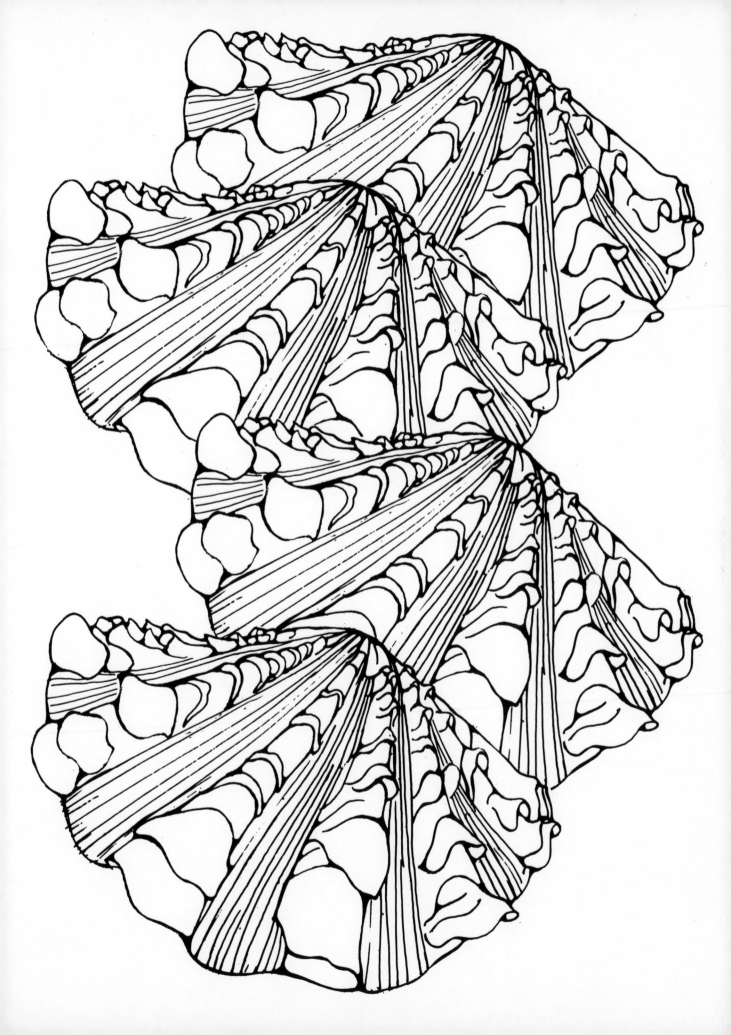

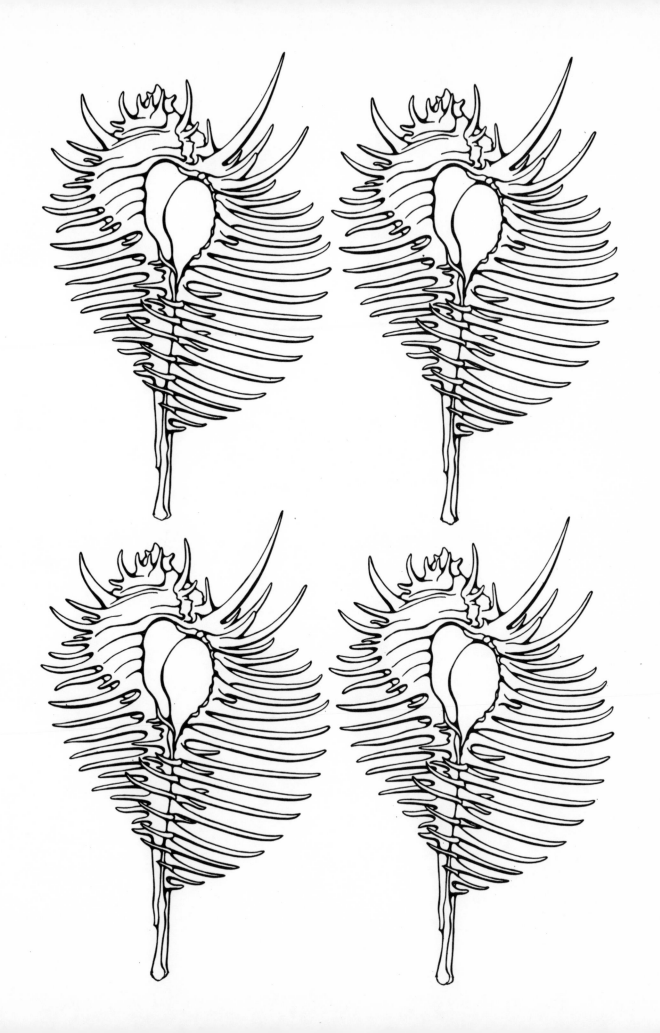

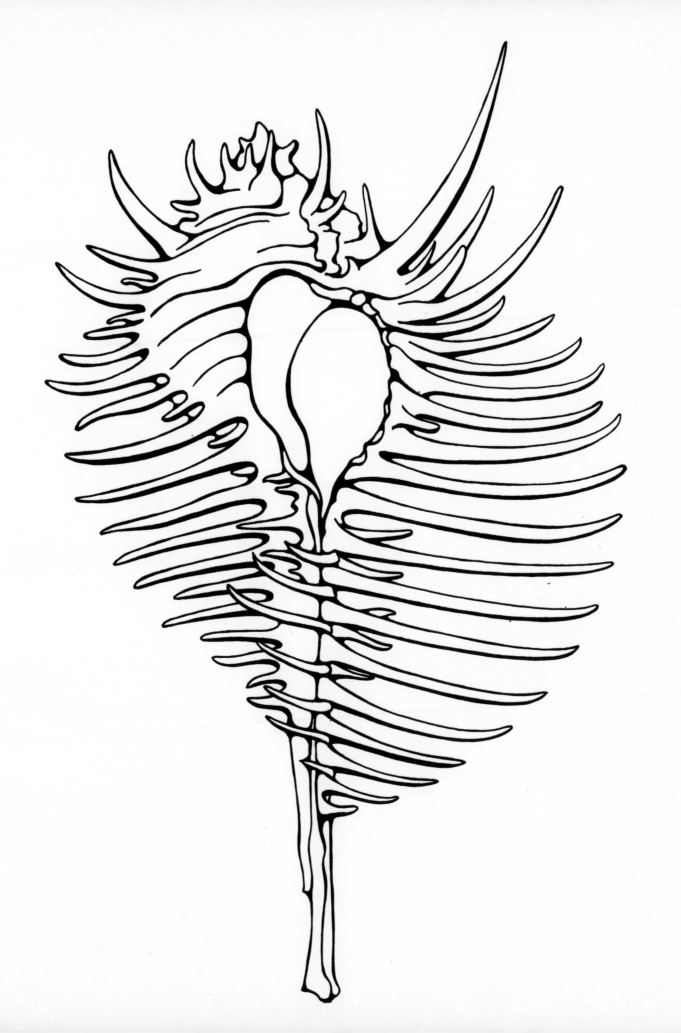

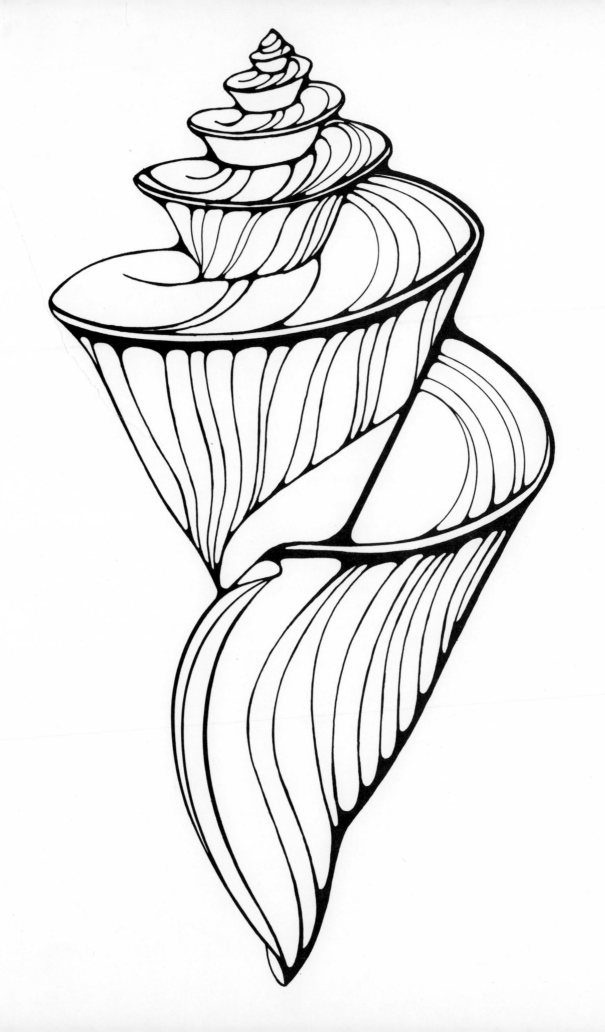

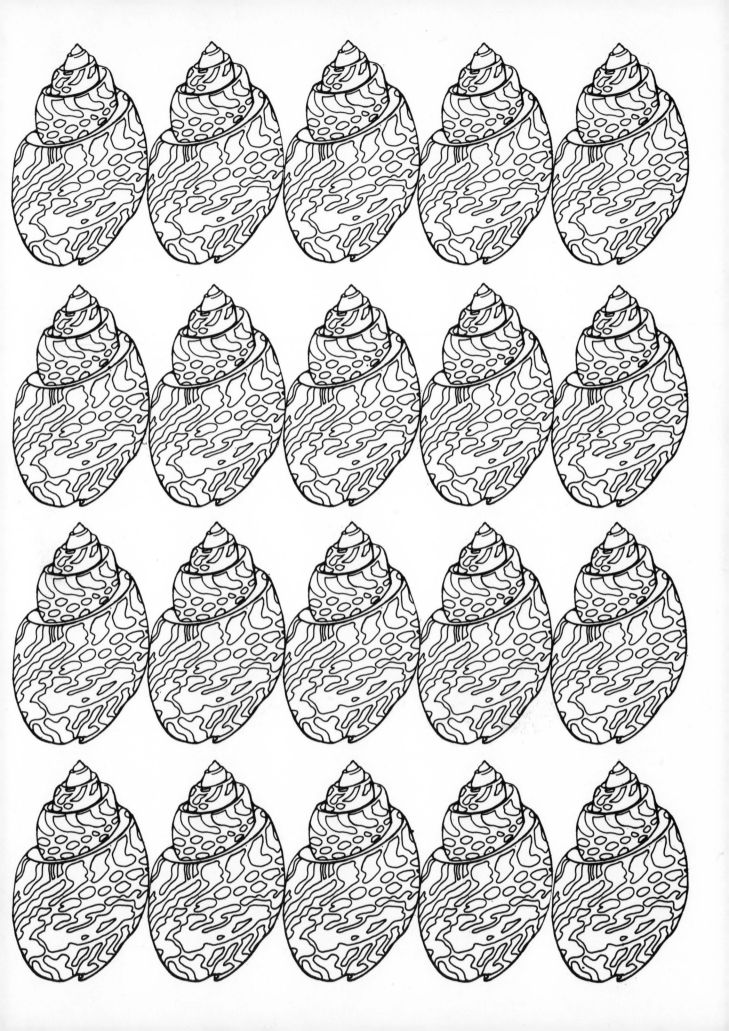

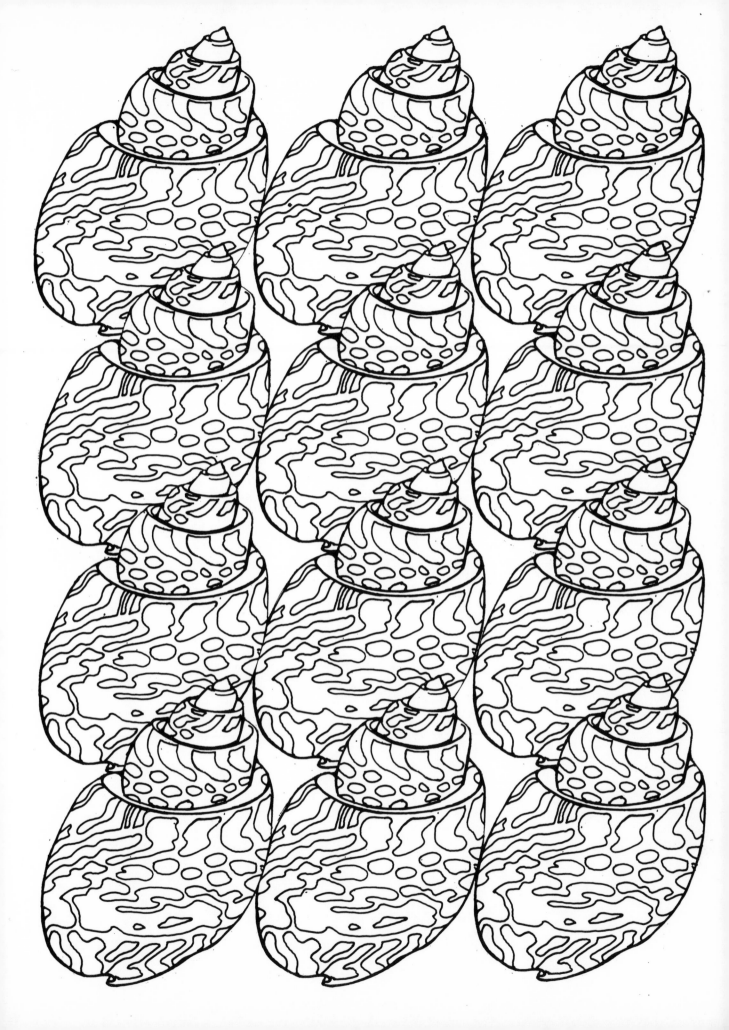

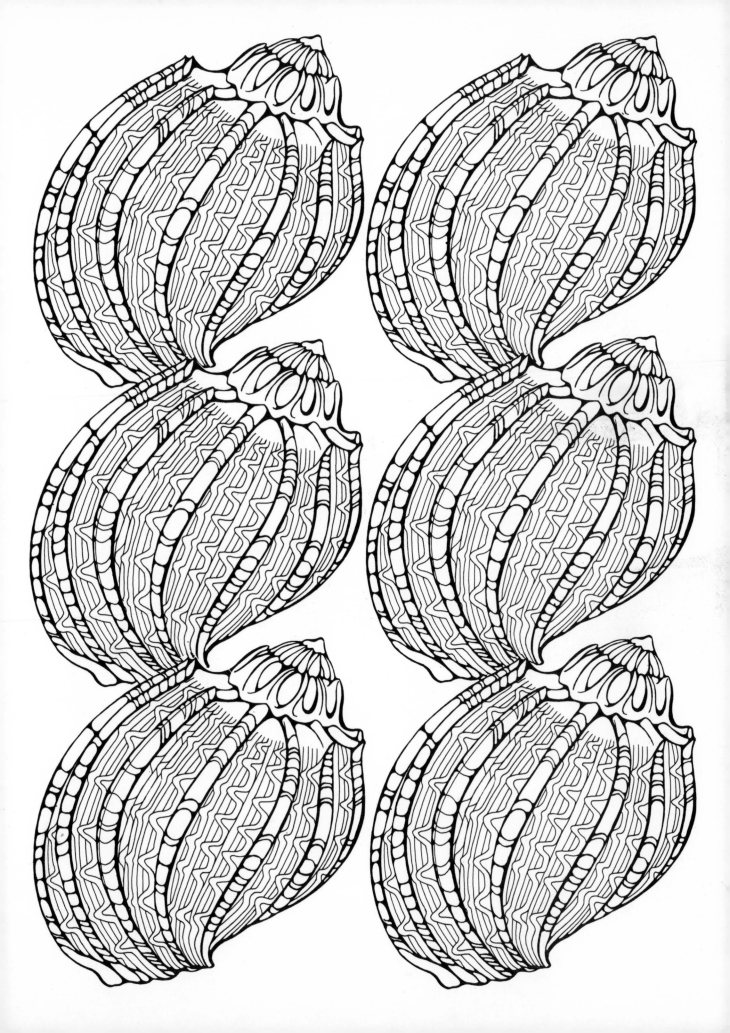

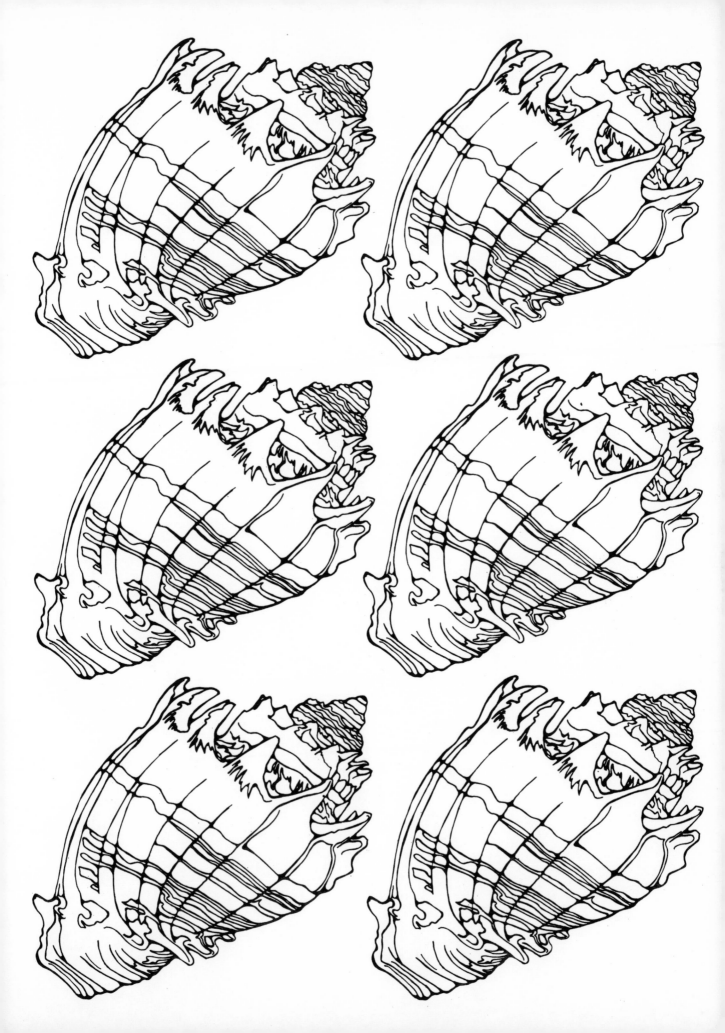